A New True Book

POLAR BEARS

By Emilie U. Lepthien

CHILDRENS PRESS ®

CHICAGO

A polar bear sleeping

To lifelong friends Edna and Richard Ansel

PHOTO CREDITS
AP/Wide World Photos—24, 25 (left)
© Reinhard Brucker—13 (right)
H. Armstrong Roberts—11 (left); © H.G.
Ross, 12; © T. Ulrich, 44
Historical Pictures Service—28 (bottom)
© Emilie Lepthien—17 (bottom left), 38 (top)
© M. Macri-Churchill, MB—23 (right), 34
(bottom right), 43 (2 photos)
North Wind Picture Archives—28 (top left),
30
Photri—38 (bottom)
Root Resources—© Anthony Mercieca
Photo, 4; © Robert W. Hutson, 23 (left), 27,
41 (bottom)
Tom Stack & Associates—© John Shaw, 7;
© W. Perry Conway, 11 (bottom right), 41
(top); © Joe McDonald, 26; © Rod Allin, 34
(top); © Mark Newman, 37
SuperStock International, Inc.—© Leonard
Lee Rue III, Cover, 6 (bottom left), 15; © Mia
and Klaus, 6 (right), 28 (top right); © Maurice
Carlisle, 25 (right)
TSW-CLICK/Chicago—© Leonard Lee Rue
III, 2; © Joe Rychetnik, 13 (left), 34 (bottom
left)
Valan—© Stephen J. Krasemann, 6 (top left),
9, 16; © Johnny Johnson, 11 (top right), 45;
© Fred Bruemmer, 14, 17 (bottom right), 19,
20 (2 photos), 33; © J.A. Wilkinson, 17 (top);
©W. Holmes, 22; © Wayne Lankinen, 36, 42
Cover: Polar bear

Library of Congress Cataloging-in-Publication Data

Lepthien, Emilie U. (Emilie Utteg)
  Polar bears / by Emilie U. Lepthien.
    p.   cm. — (A New true book)
  Includes index.
  Summary: Describes the characteristics, behavior,
and possible future of the polar bear.
  ISBN 0-516-01127-8
  1. Polar bear—Juvenile literature. [1. Polar
bear. 2. Bears.] I. Title.
QL737.C27L46 1991   91-8892
599.74'446—dc20   CIP
                                        AC

TABLE OF CONTENTS

WHAT IS A POLAR BEAR?

Some people call them "ice bears." Others call them "great white bears" or "sea bears." They are polar bears, the large, powerful hunters of the Arctic.

Long ago, some brown bears or grizzly bears may have come to the Arctic when great ice sheets covered the north. Over time, their appearance may

Polar bears (above),
grizzly bears (top left),
and brown bears (left)
are closely related.

have changed until they
became a separate group
called polar bears. However,
polar bears are still closely
related to grizzly bears
6   and brown bears.

Polar bears are at home in ice and snow.

WHERE DO POLAR BEARS LIVE?

Polar bears live in the Arctic. They like areas near the shore, where pack ice forms. They use the pack ice as seal-hunting platforms.

Between 3,000 and 4,000 polar bears live along the northern coast of Alaska. Canada has about 15,000. Polar bears are also found along the coasts of Norway and its Svalbard Islands, in Greenland, and in Siberia in the Soviet Union.

Polar bears have special features that help them to survive in the frozen north. Their creamy white fur provides good camouflage.

A polar bear's nose and mouth are black.

The bears cannot be seen easily.

Their thick fur protects them from the cold. The outer layer of fur has special guard hairs that shed water easily. Their

dense underfur protects
them from the cold.

The thick layer of
blubber, or fat, under their
skin also keeps them
warm and allows them to
go for weeks without
eating if necessary.

Polar bears shed their
winter fur and grow a
thinner summer coat that
is yellow or golden in
color. By winter they have
heavy, new white coats
again.

Polar bears have longer necks (far left) than grizzly bears (top), but their tails are short (bottom).

POLAR BEAR BODIES

The bodies, necks, and skulls of polar bears are longer than those of brown bears. They have short tails, short furry ears, and sharp teeth. Their sense of smell is so keen that they

11

can smell a seal den covered by a thick layer of snow and ice. Polar bears can hear and see about as well as human beings.

Polar bears have huge, twelve-inch front paws.

Polar bears can kill seals with one blow of their huge front paws.

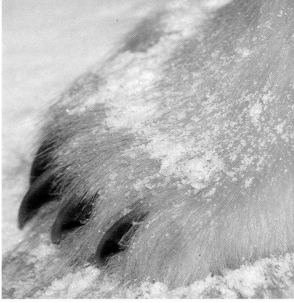

The fur on a polar bear's paw (left) helps keep the bear from slipping on ice. The claws (right) are short and thick.

Their toes are partially webbed to help them swim. Their back paws are smaller. Polar bears have pads of fur on the soles of their feet. This fur helps protect them from the cold. They have short, thick claws.

A full-grown male polar bear

Male polar bears reach their full size when they are 8 to 10 years old. Then they may measure 8 to 11 feet and weigh more than 1,000 pounds.

Female polar bears are smaller and weigh less.

Polar bears sometimes hunt reindeer on land.

WALKING

Polar bears may hunt
over 100,000 square miles
of wilderness. Their wide
paws allow them to walk
on deep snow, but they

15

A polar bear hunting for seals on the pack ice

prefer walking on ice or hard ground.

They can run at speeds up to 35 miles an hour for a short time. But they usually travel at about 2½ miles an hour.

SWIMMING

Polar bears are excellent swimmers and divers. Paddling with their front legs, they can swim 60 miles without stopping. In summer, polar bears have been found swimming in the ocean as far as 100 miles from shore.

HUNTING

Polar bears are carnivores—flesh-eating animals. They hunt seals, but will eat other animals.

Polar bears catch seals in several ways. A seal napping on an ice floe raises its head and looks

Seals are built for swimming, not for walking.

around every twenty to
thirty seconds. The hunting
polar bear "freezes" when
the seal looks around. But
when the seal drops its
head, the polar bear
inches forward again.
Finally the bear leaps

forward and grabs the seal before it can escape into the water.

Seals have breathing holes in the ice. A polar bear waits motionless for a seal to poke its nose out of the hole to breathe.

A seal at a breathing hole (below). A young polar bear (right) waits for a seal to appear.

Then the bear springs forward, kills the seal, and pulls it up through the breathing hole. This is not an easy task—the seal may weigh from 80 to 250 pounds, and the hole may be only eight to ten inches wide. But the bear keeps tugging and tugging until it has pulled the seal out.

A seal pup in its den

In spring, newborn seal
pups live in dens built
over breathing holes. The
dens are easy to find and
the pups are an easy
meal for the hungry polar
bears.

Polar bears sometimes eat
seaweed (left), but their
favorite food is seal (above).

Polar bears may feed on
a dead beached whale.
They also eat fish and
crabs. On land they eat
baby birds and bird eggs,
arctic hare, reindeer, and
plants.

POLAR BEAR CUBS

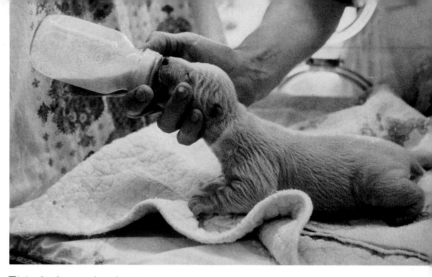

This baby polar bear was born at a zoo in Chicago.

In late October or early November, female polar bears dig dens in snowdrifts. Polar bear cubs are born in these dens. Each den has a long entrance that slopes up toward the main room. The largest dens are 8 feet wide, 10 feet long, and 3 feet high.

One or two cubs are

Polar bear cubs stay close to their mother for protection.

born between November and January. The newborn cubs are blind and hairless. They weigh only 1½ pounds. The cubs grow quickly on their mother's milk. In March or April, when they leave the den, the cubs weigh at least 20 pounds.

Nap time for this polar bear family

During their first summer,
the cubs get hunting lessons.
They go everywhere with
their mother. Most polar
bear cubs live with their
mother for one or two winters.

Polar bears are very curious animals. They examine everything strange they find. The cubs play together. Often they stand up on their hind legs and engage in a friendly boxing match.

Bear cubs like to play.

The Inuit men hunted polar bears (above) and seals (below). They used the skins from these animals to make warm clothes (right).

HUNTING THE POLAR BEAR

Long ago, the Inuit (Eskimos) used spears or bows and arrows to kill polar bears. The huge animals provided them with food and warm skins for clothing. They used the bones to make utensils. No part of the animal was wasted. The polar bear population was not threatened by the Inuits' hunting methods.

Non-native hunters brought guns to the
Arctic, and polar bears became endangered.

But when non-native
hunters arrived in the
Arctic, they used guns to
kill polar bears. They used
snowmobiles, airplanes,
and helicopters to hunt the
bears. Soon, the polar bear
was threatened with
extinction.

SAVING THE POLAR BEAR

In 1965, scientists from the five countries with lands that border the Arctic Ocean—the United States, Canada, Denmark (which owns Greenland), Norway, and the Soviet Union—held a conference. They met to discuss what was happening to the polar bears, and what could be done about it.

They found that over 1,000 bears were being

killed each year. They realized that in ten years the polar bear could be extinct. So, in 1967 the five countries signed an agreement to protect the polar bear.

The Soviets had been protecting their polar bears since 1956, but the bears traveled across Soviet borders and were killed in other countries.

After a swim, a polar bear rolls in the snow to dry its fur.

The International Union
for Conservation of Nature
and Natural Resources
(IUCN) organized a group
of scientists. These
scientists studied polar
bear migration routes. They

After polar bears are tranquilized,
scientists can fit them with radio
collars (above), weigh them on scales
attached to helicopters (below left),
and examine their teeth (below right).

counted the bears and the number of cubs born each year. Then they figured out how many polar bears could be hunted each year without threatening the bear population.

To study the movements of polar bears, scientists shoot the bears with tranquilizers. When the bears are asleep, they attach collars with radio transmitters to the animals.

Computers are able to track polar bears over the great distances they travel.

The newest bear collars transmit radio signals to the ARGOS communications satellite. The signals are then relayed to a station in France where scientists use computers to keep track of the bears.

Some bears are marked with dye. Scientists keep records of the markings so that they can follow the bears' movements.

A dye mark helps scientists track the movements of this polar bear.

Churchill, Manitoba (above), is the Polar Bear Capital of the World.
Polar bears (below) look for food in a garbage dump near Churchill.

THE TEDDY BEAR PARADE

The town of Churchill, Manitoba, on Hudson Bay in Canada, calls itself the Polar Bear Capital of the World. Churchill is on the bears' migration path. In mid-July, when the ice in Hudson Bay has melted, hundreds of polar bears pass through the town as they move inland in search of food.

Churchill is an excellent place for scientists to study polar bears. Hundreds of tourists also come to Churchill to watch the bears.

During October and November, when Hudson Bay freezes again, the migrating bears return. They walk back through Churchill in what some people call the "Teddy Bear Parade."

Tourists ride out in "tundra buggies" to safely view and photograph the polar bears. The curious polar bears wonder who the strange creatures are.

Polar bears are very
dangerous. This sign
warns people away from
a polar bear area.

Since polar bears can
be very dangerous,
Canadian schoolchildren
are taught how to avoid
an attack. Manitoba's
Department of Natural
Resources runs bear
patrols to protect people
and property.

Problem polar bears are tagged (left) and taken far away from towns.

Troublesome bears are caught, tranquilized, and tagged. Then the bears are airlifted by helicopter to seal-hunting areas where they are released.

43

THE FUTURE
OF THE POLAR BEAR

Ontario has established the Polar Bear Provincial Park to protect these magnificent animals.

Laws have been passed to protect polar bears from hunters. No more than 2

Today, polar bears are safe from hunters.

to 4 percent of the bears may be killed by Inuit. And the hunting of polar bears has been banned to all non-native hunters.

By working together, five nations in the Arctic region have saved the polar bear.

WORDS YOU SHOULD KNOW

Arctic (ARK • tik) — the far northern parts of the earth, the lands around the Arctic Ocean

blubber (BLUH • ber) — a thick layer of fat that forms under the skin of animals such as polar bears, seals, and whales

border (BOR • der) — a line that separates one country's lands from those of another country

camouflage (KAM • ah • flahj) — body coloring that makes an animal look like part of its surroundings, such as the green coloring of some insects that live in grass

carnivore (KAR • nih • vore) — a flesh-eating animal

communications satellite (kuh • myoo • nih • KAY • shuhnz SAT • il • ite) — a device sent into space by a rocket to go around the Earth sending and receiving radio signals

den (DEHN) — a warm, safe place such as a hole in the ground or a cave where an animal can rest or give birth to young

extinction (ex • TINK • shun) — dying out completely; being gone forever

ice floe (ICE FLO) — a large piece of ice that is floating in the ocean

Inuit (IN • yoo • it) — the people who have lived in the Arctic regions for thousands of years; Eskimos

migration (my • GRAY • shun) — traveling, usually for a long distance, to find more food or better weather conditions

pack ice (PACK ICE) — large areas of low ice floes floating on the ocean

population (pop • yoo • LAY • shun) — the number of animals of a certain kind that are present in an area

reserves (rih • ZERVZ) — things that are saved for later use

tranquilizers (TRAN • kwih • ly • zerz) — drugs that are sometimes used to make an animal unconscious so that scientists can examine or move the animal

INDEX

About the Author

Emilie Utteg Lepthien earned a BS and an MA degree and a certificate in school administration from Northwestern University. She taught third grade, upper grade science and social studies, and was a supervisor and principal of Wicker Park School for twenty years. Mrs. Lepthien has also written and narrated science and social studies scripts for the Radio Council (WBEZ) of the Chicago Board of Education.

Mrs. Lepthien was awarded the American Educator's Medal by Freedoms Foundation. She is a member of Delta Kappa Gamma Society International, Illinois Women's Press Association, National Federation of Press Women, Iota Sigma Epsilon journalism sorority, Chicago Principals Association, and is active in church work. She has coauthored primary social studies books for Rand, McNally and Company and served as educational consultant for Encyclopaedia Britannica Films.